DOUBTER'S HYMNAL

DOUBTER'S HYMNAL

Laura Cok

Mansfield Press

Library and Archives Canada Cataloguing in Publication

Title: Doubter's hymnal / Laura Cok.
Names: Cok, Laura, author.
Description: Poems.
Identifiers: Canadiana 2019010239X | ISBN 9781771262088 (softcover)
Classification: LCC PS8605.O3793 D68 2019 | DDC C811/.6—dc23

Cover Image: A Young Lady Writing in a Hymnal by Giacomo Pacchiarotto
Author Photo: Mike Meehan
Design: Denis De Klerck

The publication of *Doubter's Hymnal* has been generously supported by
the Canada Council for the Arts and the Ontario Arts Council.

Mansfield Press Inc.
25 Mansfield Avenue, Toronto, Ontario, Canada M6J 2A9
Publisher: Denis De Klerck
www.mansfieldpress.net

For Vicki Verhulst Cok
and
Dennis Cok

TABLE OF CONTENTS

NOAH'S WIFE

I can breathe through storms but this rain
will not stop, drum-drumming on the roof
till the animals howl their throats raw.
Everywhere creatures,
feathers in my teeth, I tell him
I don't understand:
What are we to eat?
Not these.

God does not speak to me.
I saw my neighbour's child
curled with branches, water rising
above roofs, and we with it.
Some shift of the earth;
some breaking of the sea.
My husband speaks of wonders, but
he does not speak to me.

This is a God to be bargained with,
who saves my sons and presses
the neighbours' faces into the water,
a divine hand at the backs of their necks.
I do not want to be saved.
I do not want to be good.

CELERYVILLE

At ten he could not tell
endive from romaine, lettuce from weed,
as he bent, obedient, down rows
of rising mist and celery,
naming plants that would raise agony
if it weren't for the sleeves
to his wrists in the summer heat.

Tugged from the earth,
celery-trimmed, lettuce-dipped,
they came clean into waiting arms
like the noontime children immersed and
born again into radish leaves.

ABSOLUTION

I would never confess
how she felt like a punishment
and afterwards I swore to be a better man:
up all night with my sleepless daughter,
her twisting body held against my chest.

At 3 a.m. I took my marriage vow.
I would not see you again.
The hours before my wedding
I kissed you in the parking lot;
I laid you down in the truck bed.
Then I married a woman in a white dress
and buried myself in the layers and layers of her.

But God is cruel and does not forgive.
Even while I lay beside you he was working,
my daughter only the size of my thumb
within her mother, her spine twisting,
her brain... This far you may go
and no farther.

You spoke of angels among us
who walk undetected.
This is not that kind of story.

MISCARRIAGE

The secret daughter is murderous.
She who lived in my mother's womb
before me, who made it her graveyard and bed.
She is the sacrifice
to my petty god, who demanded
life, blood, a tangle of cords and veins.

Once I tried to follow
this stranger with my name.
I saw how I could let myself dissolve,
slip out by slow turns of the moon.
She took me by the heel
and reeled me in, like a silvery fish.
But there is always a price to pay.

She came into the world with me,
my older twin, bloody double.
She is not who you think, this child
that you bore. Her heart
shines like a knife.

THE STRANGE HOUSE

The swirl of a drunken room is
the shape childhood rolls towards:
a great and gleaming kitchen, the gentle clink
of silverware and wine glasses. There are other children
but you do not know them. The backyard
smells of cedar where the bark and soil
have been freshly turned and turned. Fish
on the walls of the bathroom, a plate
shattering on the floor, a long way away.

In the next room there are grown-up voices,
involved in the incomprehensible business
of being grown, then lower
and talking about things you don't understand
until later, turning them over in your mind.
While the voices drift towards their owners
you walk from room to room,
touching everything, wanting to see
what stays solid and what you had only ever dreamed.

THE PIANO TEACHER

When I was young I dreamed of opera halls.
I'd take my seat behind the baby grand,
draped all in velvet, so as not to shine
too brightly, or distract the voyeur's eye
away from centre stage. I had no wish
for stardom, spotlights, roses in my arms
from an adoring throng. I wished to be
the heartbeat of the thing, the steady line
they'd only notice if it were not there.
I'd hold the music in my pulsing blood.

I practiced. I advanced. Then married young.
My oldest daughter just turned twenty-two,
and she is still a child. But youth will have
its way, and I had mine. At first I played
in concerts, locally at least, and then
my own recital. The reviews
were positive, though all made sure to note
my housewife status. Older times;
they half-expected curlers in my hair.
I didn't hold another, not alone.

I started playing churches, when their own
small congregations lacked sufficient skill.
The income helped. My husband lost his job.
I started teaching lessons on the side.
Soon I had twenty students, guiding
fingers to their chords, one hand around
my baby's head, to help her as she drank.
Such was the benefit of teaching there
at home. Peace settled over lessons as
my husband kept his quiet in the yard.

He had a temper, worse when unemployed.
I swear he never laid a hand on me,
but smashed the dishes, punched the screen,
and threatened once to overturn
the whole piano, bench and hammers all.
He's mellowed, now, with age. I'm teaching yet.
My students don't grow old, just cycle through.
Sometimes when they're still mangling Für Elise
I wish he'd done it. Turned it upside down,
the dying crash like thunderous applause.

MOTHER'S DAY, 1988

That morning, the blood—

and now he is speaking of God's gifts,
bestowed on womankind, pain
in childbearing, and pain when they leave

but a gift entire, let us bow
and pray and thank the Father
that he has given us all these mothers—

and she thinks, you know nothing of it,
men in their pulpits with gravel in their mouths

for two months she'd tried to hold onto me
but even as she sat in church listening
I was slipping away

with the dreams she had, restless, my face
only a suggestion of a child

she could teach me piano, I would love God
as she did, baptismal water running through my hands

and there's an end to it, she thought,
this third time, not knowing yet
how I could cling on, tucked into her body
until I left her, a thousand times over

in the apricot orchard she could no longer hear his voice
my shadow giggled and pulled the hard green fruit from the trees

AWAKE

Sometimes I have to howl but others
you're at my bedside already, peering through
the wooden slats. Animals surround me,
anatomically inaccurate: pink bear, Velcro penguin.

In my dreams, I could stand; run, even,
with your hands flapping at my back like worried birds.
It wasn't anything I'd thought about beforehand
or stumbled toward: just me, running.

Other times I dream the pink bear to life
or that you will not be there when I wake
and I'll be there, screaming, while the sheets turn gray.
While the earth moves and cracks.

You are still inscrutable to me, what it is
precisely that you want. For me to be quiet,
for me to sleep, then with the same urgency
to wake. Have I learned to stand in your dreams?

Do you dream? I saw you sleep, once,
from my vantage point beneath your chin.
I could have rolled away from you then
but I did not. Can you know

what is coming, that each night
my hands grip the bars, my soft feet flex, my knees
already practicing their straighten, and my heart
practicing its close.

HE LOVES THE TREES THAT DON'T LOVE BACK

He loves the trees but they don't love him back.
Up in the mountains, the lakes are like glass.
He loves the trees. He climbs up the mountain.
He carries his daughter halfway on his back.

Halfway up the mountain he rests by a rock.
His daughter drinks water. Her eyes are like glass.
There is a god, who lives in the trees.
He prays to be worthy, that God loves him back.

He carried the water here to the mountain.
His daughter believes in the god of the trees.
He loves her and loves her. The trail cuts like glass
up the side of the mountain, and halfway to God.

His daughter stands at the top of the mountain.
Her thirst is for something she doesn't name God.
She loves him and loves him. The trees are his own.
The lakes fill with water. His daughter drinks glass.

He carries his daughter. They rest by a rock.
The weight of his daughter remembers his back.
The water he carried loves only the lakes.
The mountains remember the weight of the trees.

EARTHQUAKE

There are some things that can't stay as they are.
Screws loosen, doors unlatch, the wind swings wide
through empty cabins where the family's car
has rumbled off. The apron strings, untied,
flap lonely on the lawn; their edges fray.
That child you swing in circles, round and round,
will lengthen, darken, and wake up one day
as someone else. His hallway footsteps sound
peculiar to your ear. Whole cities shift
and settle, sink a fraction of an inch
while you can barely bring yourself to lift
your eyes to his, afraid that you might flinch.
The earth unravels. Mountains heave and sway.
You want to reach him, touch him, make him stay.

CHERUB

For punishment her father made her wear
a sweatshirt, nothing underneath.
This was California, so you can imagine.

All day she grew warmer and warmer
but couldn't take it off,
her round face sweating.

She told me once she'd had a vision of angels—
or not a vision, she had seen them, wide awake,
in the laundry room down the hall.

Treacherous child, I asked her mother
for the truth of it. They were very religious.
So was my family, but a different kind, without visions.

The mother said yes, it was true.
There were angels, standing by a pile of unwashed clothes,
slowing burning from the inside out.

THINGS WE LOST

Next week I am moving away, but tonight
we are two paper cranes
folded into a wooden swing.
Your dusty feet scuff the ground.

My brother, younger, knows nothing
of goodbyes; he only cries
when he slips on gravel,
but swallows words like candy.

Grape soda runs sticky down your arms,
thin like bird bones, though I
am the one with wings.
My brother shrieks in the pool

as his friends douse him with water.
A baptism, phoenix rising.
Tonight you are full of ash,
gray-faced, volcano-eyed.

Dark settles and sings.
Next the flashlights,
which dissect the air
and catch my brother leaping,

held up in the weighted air,
gleaming like a firefly.

REDWOOD CAMP

We lifted our eyes to the hills,
the small cabins and the redwood trees.

In the evenings we sang
and the sound drifted out through the open doors.
Jesus was as real to me as water.

My mother and I sat together,
pairs huddled around the campfire.

When it was her turn she said she was most proud of me
for joining them at the table, for breaking bread.

Of all my life, what mattered most.
I lifted my eyes to the hills.

My mother and I stood together
to receive water, to wash her feet,
which I could not bring myself to touch.

I knew then
I was not what she wanted.

CARDIOLOGY

The murmuring curtain of my brother's heart
let the wrong blood in, the unsanctified
slipping past to the holiest of holies.

All the church prayed, and I thought: how glamorous,
a brother with a hole in his heart.
I jumped rope for his sake. I bent my ear to his tiny chest.

When he counts to two the image grows clear.
The man behind the curtain has patched it up
and when it grows it will not buckle at the seams.

When I was a child I believed in God and thanked him.
A long time ago. That does not mean it was not a miracle,
the whirr and tick of his mathematical heart.

THE APOSTLES

Each of them vies to be the favourite,
for that holy hand to pass

briefly over the tops of their heads
as though they're feverish children.

Of course they've seen it done,
seen the heat lift from the cheeks,

the necks untwist, the pallor fade,
word passing from village to village—

but to *feel* it, the new blood and clearer eyes
and a mouth that will not stop singing

a separate miracle entire, the ease
of finally believing what they see and see.

IT COMES NEAR

When you lived in Africa
the rock formations loomed up
like the playthings of giants.
You thought of the Psalms, of the
Valley of the Shadow of
Death. Surely this was it, this
unknown place where your husband
clambered, could so easily
fall. Silk-sweet like seduction,
darkly beautiful, untamed.

This morning you found him on
a couch in the living room,
one shoe off, his glasses gone.
He didn't know where he was.
When the nurses came to help,
you studied the bed, immense
and devouring, a chair,
heart monitor keeping time:
these things daily like the walls
and so exquisitely strange.

THE MISSIONARY'S SON

It wasn't like they say it was. The bright
blank dust when we walked to class, the snake's head
chopped off with a hoe: all this was true enough.
My father taught chemistry and religion.
The other children's parents were farther,
their summers marked by planes like the tin roofs
they rose above. And once it was like that
for me, when I was small, and my brother
before me, while my sisters cried and cried.
I learned to go away, and learned it well.

My wife has called this childhood trauma.
She says leaving my parents so often
gave me a fear of abandonment. But
what she doesn't understand: I left them.
I wouldn't wave from the window of the plane.
In the summers I moved awkwardly through
the bones of the house, that pointed embrace.
But why should I love them more? When I knew
at the end of the sharp dry summer,
a small tin plane, and school again, and again.

Nobody beat me, and nobody crept
to my room in the insect-laden night.
The worst is what I tell my daughter when
she scorns her dinner: how every Wednesday
they fed us sauerkraut, and every time
I vomited. They didn't believe me,
punishments passed out like they were something
sustaining, something to clamber over,
reach higher, grow less lonely in the end.
My child, I will never make you eat.

We never starved, though I suppose some did.
Those of us who never went home did so
for reasons less glamorous, unlikely
to appear on WorldVision. Pneumonia,
for one. He was ten. In the States
he would have grown old, here in the tropics,
my small friend, his small grave. When I came back
to visit, nearly three decades later,
his stone was still there. His bones never left.
Perhaps we were wrong to have come to this land.

My daughter thinks so. She cringes in class,
watching anthropological films,
reading books on colonialism,
wanting no part in the faith that brought us
to that dark continent. We weren't the first:
Johanna before us had set up the church.
She rests there as well, is honoured, revered,
both there and at home. With no wish to harm,
arriving to teach in a place prepared,
we could not have destroyed so very much.

Of course there are rumours. There always will be.
The whispers, the footnotes, the mosquito
in the ear, the netting pushed aside
to let them in. They say they let them in.
I don't believe them. I never saw it
there, in my school, a night not electric,
there was not so much harm done to us
or this hot bright land. The fighting goes on,
as it will. And people do terrible
things. The truth stays there, coiled like a snake.

AUGUST 1959, ZAKI BIAM, NIGERIA

It's been three Sundays since we saw you last.
Our journey here was pleasant, thank the Lord;
the children travelled well. Today the rest
is compound-wide. The children, though, were bored
throughout the sermon, which was an hour
long, and in a language we know nothing of.
The pews cement, thatched roof and muddy floor,
no doors or windows. But we felt the dove
move through that place. The brush of feathery wings
against our shoulders. And despite their stares
(we're noticeably foreign) when we sing
it's as one family asking for your prayers.
The worship's half familiar, halfway strange.
The tune's familiar, but the words have changed.

THE CALLING

what they told us was
open your hearts
to His leading
His arms nailed open

batter my heart, oh

but I do not want to go
to the jungles of Borneo
or some desert wasteland
with grit in my eyes

and this meant I was bad
when it was so simple
all I had to do was say yes

yes to the bended knee
yes to the bread and wine

He would set a path before me
and when I grew up I would not depart from it
I would not
go, I would not

His eyes on the sparrow
without blinking
the sparrow answering the call
and response, the call, the quiet trill

there is always a man
with a dove and a golden key

and I am praying that
God forget me
that he let me become a mote
in someone else's eye

THEOLOGY

We have never escaped from Eden.
A thousand thousand years gone by
with the leaves decaying
and even the redwoods grown weary
of their bulk, the streaks of blood
that tinge their bark.

Here still are a woman and a man.
Each morning he tells her
the story of her birth
and his flesh torn open.
He takes her hand
and places it on the space between his ribs.
Here, he says, and I was so happy
when you appeared—
though she hears the accusation
whistle out between his bones.

Even when she climbs her tree
she can't see to the edge of things.
Fruit breaks open across her world,
stupefying and sweet. The vines
catch at her feet. The flaming arm
that guards the gate is his.

NUMBERS

I got stuck at Numbers, where the tot and bale
were divvied up to God, families, girl children dead
last. I'd soldiered through Leviticus
with steel and legalistic glee, where God set balanced
weights on the side of justice. But Numbers
was just columns of arithmetic and I thought that the girl in my class
who claimed to have read the whole Bible was probably lying,
and lying was a sin, but the seventh time they counted seven years
I wanted to sleep for seven hours.

I'd read the parts with Jesus in them, of course,
and all the exciting bits: Jonah and the whale,
Noah and the flood. It was enough to make a girl
seek out dry land. But I thought He'd love me more
once I read it all the way through
and I thought I would understand it then:
what everyone else seemed already to know.
But Jesus spoke of numbers too:
How many times must you forgive?
Seventy times seven. And still I'm trying.

EARLY HOUR

In order to accommodate the schedules
of particularly demanding students
one section of American Literature
will begin at 6:55 a.m.

No, that wasn't quite right. The demanding
student. The schedule that's demanding:
a foreign language, advanced band,
where I'd sit in the front row
wearing a callus into my lower lip
with my teeth. A quarter turn
and I could almost see her:
focused, blonde, the duck's mournful call.

We were all of us demanding students.
Bleary at the edges, half unpopular,
half hiding the secret of their ambition.
Guess which half was me.
But surprise: I had a secret too.
Slowly we moved in our different orbits.
Two seats ahead of me and to the left,
a flash of light hair.

First, cereal in the kitchen, faint light.
My dad rising as early each morning.
Then I would drive the lumbering minivan,
marking down each ten-minute increment.
Grapefruit split in half, no sugar.
Love is an early riser. Sometimes
it moves through the dark so quietly
you're still too asleep to see.
I came to know that road so well
I could have driven it with my eyes closed.

In her classroom there were packets
of hot chocolate, tea, instant coffee for the brash.
I didn't know my own luck. All of us
were demanding. She gave me printouts
of her favourite poems, where days stacked like teacups.
Sometimes I stopped listening, curled into my desk,
planning my tiny betrayals, waiting for the sun to rise.

BLUES FOR HELEN OF TROY

We've all known girls like Helen, cheerleading outfits on—
the captain of the football team takes photos on the lawn.
We find her floating naked in a backyard pond.

We've all known girls like Helen, girls whose beauty leads to fame,
and when they're on the billboards, their own innocence they'll claim.
They're traded off like baseball cards and not to blame.

And all these girls like Helen, they'll be lovely, maybe kind;
the rest of us will bite our lips and say that we don't mind.
You'll believe us only if you're deaf and blind.

Sometimes the girls like Helen take a razor to their skin,
then they fill the tub with water and climb right in.
Or else they do it slowly, and just grow thin.

A thousand girls like Helen have a thing or two to learn;
the ships arrive and make the oceans froth and churn.
They lean outside their windows and we watch them burn.

STONES

That summer I worked on a farm
in southern Ontario, where every year
after the frost and thaw, the heaving land
coughed up stones by the bucketful

which is how we took them back again:
rows of tin buckets like ragged teeth
lined up along the hill, paint-worn
and dented with the weight of the stones

we dropped in. A heavy percussion
marked by the bruises against my thighs
when the lip of the bucket swung too close,
and the rust creased along the lines of my palm

where a fortune-teller might study the curve and fall,
tell me the date I'd fall in love or
the meandering map of my life—
not like this, row by row, bending at the sight

of stones glittering up, catching half-melodies
from the women alongside, hearing
but not understanding their conversation:
a world I am too young to inhabit

but can feel myself on the edge of.
We ride back to the house in the last light
cradled in the gaping mouth of the tractor,
my legs dangling out where they tuck theirs in,

mine thin and brown, unmarked by children
and houses and late-night calls when you already know
what the news is, must be, at that hour—still apart,
still jolted over stones we've gathered and then laid down.

LEVITICUS

All night I sit and watch her and I burn.
My skin grows dark with rising hate and blood
but hate's a lie by half. I watch her mouth,
don't think about it, I don't think of her,
I think of God the Father, Jesus Christ,
begotten of the Virgin, without sin.

I want to know: to touch her, is it sin?
The men of God all tell me that I'll burn
not knowing they mean me and mean my god
who offered up a sacrifice of blood.
I'd make the sacrifice again for her,
would let the crows come, have my eyes and mouth.

She wouldn't understand the words I'd mouth,
the promises I never gave for sin.
She didn't want it. Still it was for her,
the throat scraped raw from screaming, fingers burned,
the girl's fool heart that pumped my brackish blood,
a sacrifice to other women's gods.

Still I believed in her and in their God
who had a hungry all-consuming mouth.
It couldn't get enough of children's blood
so sent them into flesh and bid them sin.
How beautiful a hell must be. The burn
the way she never touched me, and how her

hands brushed against my own in chapel. Her
God was a kinder one. He was a god
regretting that he'd let his people burn,
who watched the flames melt their distorted mouths.
From birth I'd known that I was drenched in sin,
and it was only quieted by blood.

I gave a year of sacrificial blood;
I would have given more for sake of her.
The scars a knot, the knot untied a sin.
What can he want from me, my mother's god?
The prayers all taste of copper in my mouth.
All night I sit and watch her and I burn.

I pray to blood, my vengeful vanished God,
the taste of her, bright apples in my mouth,
give sweetness to my sin and let me burn.

FRUIT

even the peaches
in their wooden bowl
would like to shrug off
their loosening jackets and

let the sun beating down
on the kitchen table
overheat
their bare flesh

to a sticky embrace
and sweet decay

THE DIVORCE

I was not ready for it when it happened
despite watching it gather
in the distant fields for many years.
Then it grew closer the way a thunderstorm
rolls in over the prairies. You could be standing
on your own front porch watching the greenish underbellies of the clouds
slowly boiling towards you and still be surprised
when it's your house they choose to stand over,
your own roof pelted with hail. And the crop
you planted with your own hands, grown from nothing—
do you regret it, seeing what's come?
But who could live that way—seeing the fields barren.
And there are other disasters greater. This
is what it means to be human, and foolish—
watching the storms gather and spit in the sky,
still believing they will, like God's avenging spirit, pass you by.

TELEKINESIS

When I was a child
I could close the door to my bedroom
just by looking at it. I could rumple
my bed to make it appear
as though I'd slept through the night.

For a while at school it kept me safe,
then made me a target.
I could move a desk with my mind
but that was no match
for a strong arm, crumpled lunch bag, ill will.

It would have been unfair to take up sports
so I didn't. I ran long distances
through the woods behind my house.
Ahead of me the path would clear
but my body demanded the work.

Slowly it slipped out of me, with practice.
To make even a sound I have to reach out my hand,
lift a pencil, let it fall.

THE BIRD GIRLS

That was the year they'd call the night before
like birds that congregate on black phone wires
to plan what they'd wear to school the next day:
skirts, though it was a deathly winter there.

They were all spindly knees and feathered hips,
and wore their straight blonde hair like nestled crowns
for their higher births and older money,
last names emblazoned across the city.

Once a friend of mine overheard in time
to wear hers. We viewed it as betrayal,
in our jeans without affiliation,
without thigh-skimming pleats, without a guard

against talons. And without brighter wings
they didn't yet know couldn't bear their weight.

THE PRIEST

The chalice filled with blood is not the wine
that we would drink in restaurants and bars.
We never sat too close. You were not mine.
Each time we left and headed for our cars.
You don't know why I'm here, or even where.
The wine, the talk—it all became obscene
and I could not remain. I didn't dare.
And then God's promises, my soul wiped clean.
I'll be ordained tomorrow. You won't come
to see me write the poems of wine and bread.
You wouldn't know the words. You'd have to hum.
And I will have to marry Christ instead.
I'll pour the wine, a red and holy flood,
but love, it's never wine, it's always blood.

DESIRE LINES

The paths cut cross for those who wander late
inanimate, insensible to leaves
piled up along the side of well-worn paths
while others go the long way round,
with cobwebbed eyes, delirious and drowned.
Define the damp from every upturned
underbellied rock. Desire bids us come
and follow, twisting at its silver stalk.
The darker forest, trees that wind and snatch
and feet cut short through Douglas fir. Let catch
the wind, let ghosts of other walkers guide.
And soon the slide of animals to lakes,
the change like fog that takes on flesh. These berries
taste of gin, and juniper, and strange.

PAINTING OF A PHOTOGRAPH

One building didn't swallow the other
but grew up inside it, shouldering into the courtyard
like a child learning to operate the man's hands
that have suddenly appeared at the end of his arms.

In the motel's embrace there were doors, windows, passageways—
without the need for breathing room
for these are modern times.

When it came down you could still see the marks
like my brother's dirty handprint when he jumped
and touched the ceiling overhead
too high for my mother to reach.
Clean edges where the doors have been.
Dirtier bricks. A windowsill clinging on, improbably,
like a mollusk.

At first you think you're looking at an interior, a ruined home laid bare.
But at the top of the canvas, a sprinkling of snow in white paint.
Then the chill comes over you.

BENEDICTION

The first days were a cathedral of legs and arms,
his ribs the high arched ceiling, my blood
the sacramental wine. The dark pooled along his collarbone
when he turned his face away. We were the first
and holiest religion, and my skin was a psalm
set to music and sung, his mouth
at the roots of my hair and a bow drawing tight
across my thin blue veins. Of all the hymns
I still swear some of them were true.

All along he thought I was someone else.
My body transformed, shot through with gold,
far more beautiful than I was before. And my soul
he could cup in his palms, still believing
it was something he could keep.
I became miserly, clutching my widow's mite
to my hollow chest.

My face was still my own.
My legs, my bones.
My heart closed against him like a fist.

In the last days we touched
like there were knives pressed to our skins:
carefully, so as not to be splayed and laid bare.
Our bodies so imperfectly designed,
blood just under the surface, ready at any moment
to be sacrificed to some greater god.

He wanted me to swear never
to write about him, the same fight
over and over again, because what do I own

of my own life and his,
and what do I owe him afterwards and now,
and how many promises can I break
with my deaf and terrible heart?

WHAT COUNTS WHAT STICKS

Geometry: the angle of elbow to nose,
what could be broken if you'd really tried.
Can you tell yourself now you really tried?
How about the first or the second or the third?

If you shout and push it's almost unequivocal
unless he thinks you're joking,
unless he thinks the smile on your face
means both of you are having fun. Have you
ever seen an animal lift its lips?
My fangs fell out when I was still a child.

Lying still won't cut it, protestations neither,
since it's always a matter of degree.
The whole thing counts, probably, but what about
half, or half again, or just the pressure
of a rubber band about to snap—

not if you took your pants off yourself,
not if you could still breathe under his weight,
not if you loved him.

EPISTLE

It's winter still. Last week
it snowed. A year ago
walking around in shorts,
this year's ice overlaid
like plastic wrap. You
can still see through it,
preserved, sealed. I suppose
there's not much ice where you are.
(You see, I can still make jokes.)
I don't wish you were here.
Peel off enough layers
and all you find is freezer burn.
To post this letter
I'll have to close the door.

ARSONIST

When he touched me
the knife slipped—
flames spilling from my finger.
I burnt my mouth with its heat.
　　　—"*Paul,*" Lorna Crozier

My thumb grew warm from trying,
metal-ridged, chemically pure.
He cupped his hand around his mouth,
smoke sweet and tangled
from that first long breath.
He liked that I couldn't spring it free,
the flame: men like to teach me
what to do.
Ashes settled on my knee.
When he touched me

I let him.
My arms grew like ivy
around his throat. The words
went between us
on the edge of a blade.
The walls had been stripped
of paint, the bones showing through.
When he called me beautiful
like he was reading a script
the knife slipped—

took a layer of skin, me some
new pink glistening thing.
The wind left nothing raw,
I was armored in flesh, how it rushed
through the world to these small rooms
in the sky, the whiskey-voiced singer

from the corner speakers. He took
my hand, curled it into a fist,
then flicked the lighter, let it linger,
flames spilling from my fingers.

He admired my helplessness,
thought I wasn't a danger to him.
There are other ways and secret
arsonists. My fingers matchsticks,
my bones kindling. Without looking
I stepped into the street.
He stood at the other side, waiting.
I lowered my lips to the salt
at his throat. Then the beat.
I burnt my mouth with its heat.

BIRDS OF CATHEDRALS

It must happen all the time—the dip and fall,
dark flit of a bird through the eaves,
unpanicked, unperturbed, the great marble pillars
with shadows of branches and leaves made strange.

The builders had been half-crazed, ruin over ruin,
begging attention—these piles of stones,
this volume of air. Ramp after ramp,
close enough for God to see his face.

The bird narrowed through a hole in the ceiling
three hundred feet up, whole and holy,
and it was not stealing bits of gold leaf to adorn its nest,
and it was not pausing to gaze at the face of the Christ child,
and whether I were there to mark its sudden wing
and flutter, it cared not, neither did it spin.

FLORENCE

The girl was hurrying across the square
sun-toasted, not yet drunk, still afternoon,
hair long and loosed, half blank, skirt short, legs bare
towards endless halls of paintings, room by room.

A man was standing in her way, a clown
or something, twenty tourists in the stands,
he flipped her skirt up, quickly flipped it down;
the crowd laughed at the humor of his hands.

The girl kept walking forward like a shark
who has to keep on moving or she'll choke.
The offices, the paintings, quiet dark.
The tourists laughed. It was a funny joke,

she guessed, the sudden shock of air and sun.
She looked at every painting, one by one.

SLEEPING BEAUTY

Like most stories, they got it wrong.
She was napping, not cursed;
the malignant fairy nothing more
than a worrier. It would be so easy

for her to fall and hurt herself
and so there were cushions everywhere,
plush rugs, soft food, carpet even on the ceiling,
all sound and singing swaddled.

The prince is an afterthought.
He'd probably gotten lost. He kissed her.
Then the needle.
Then the blood.

SAME OLD STORY

nowhere in the book
did they talk of dragging hours
and a sense of nearest misses
and the scent of rotting flowers
leaving their trace
and the wet unwanted kisses
and the hands on your face
as he took and he took

where have my old
protectors gone
the bears and all the wild things
and where is Max, his paper crown,
his claws and teeth
his dinner warm

he said, I like
when you say no

and where was Miss Clavel
appearing in the hush of night
appearing like a warning bell
to tell me Something
is not right

a flattened couch
on New Year's Eve
and he was aping nice
like Alice and her tiny gifts
he gave me something filled with ice
Drink me, he said,
stay off the floor
there's room to stay with me
in bed

and nowhere Alice in my head
to wake me up
to shut the door

but where's the beast
and where is Belle
to change the ending
raise the dead
and couldn't it be pleasanter at least
to tell

LITANY

There are things I have to keep learning over and over again:
how wanting something is never enough.
I'm not a fool, understand, but I'm not special either.
I tried all of the usual tricks. Stripped to the waist
I met his eyes. He told me I was beautiful,
as though he thought I wasn't paying attention.
But I was always paying attention.

There were nights he wrapped me in his arms.
There were days I laid my head on his shoulder.
We never spoke about what was or wasn't between us.
That's what let me believe it was real.

There was one morning, on my roommate's couch,
I answered work emails and spoke on the phone. While I wasn't looking
he played with the very ends of my hair
as though he thought there was a part of my body
he could touch where it wouldn't hurt.

SECONDLY

Let there be nothing between us. Let all
the glances slide back, silent in their grooves.
Return to the shelf every warm palm that
slides against my hips, every salty lick
to the whorl behind your ear. Let there be
no bars, no bathrooms; let us teetotal.
Let me never drop my clothes to the floor
defiant, knowing you'll never touch me
by sun or the twinkle lights I've strung.
No phones. No coffee. No mutual friends.
Leave me unkissed and uncared for and wanting.
Leave me that one thing. Don't take me dancing,
let us be strangers to one another.
I am begging you. I am begging you.

THE DANGERS

Sometimes you sense them,
the maybes that flutter around your life.
They are spread across continents, a few
in every city, and you believe
if you stood still enough in any one place
one might alight upon your hair.

They are the men you might have loved
but for time, circumstance, geography.
One you saw through the subway window,
pulling out of Bathurst station, you standing
there on the platform as useless as a pigeon.
One you met at a party while his girlfriend
ate cheese spread on small crackers, elegantly.
You felt the crackle of it
like a downed wire.

It is a dangerous thing. They do not know
to keep out of each other's way
and are forever popping up
at inopportune times: when you're
trying to see a movie.
When you're already married.
When it's Valentine's Day, you're alone
in a dark bar, and know better.

But don't you—seeing the spark jump
from the live wire to the puddle of dirty rain

with its miraculous oily sheen—
want to reach out your palm, and take it?

SEX TOURIST IN THAILAND

I know I live an enviable life.
Each day, each morning breaks upon my arms
and some new lovely girl. Though I say girl
please know that no one here is underage
or so they tell me. Who am I to say?
But lovely, young, consenting to be touched,
professing adoration to my face.
Enough to turn a man's head quite around.
How envious of me they all must be,
how sick to hear my gloating. Nights at clubs
and mornings at the beach. Black hair, white skin;
compliant, supple, understanding, young.

Of cannibals it's said they ate the flesh
that they might never die, for eating life
subsumed the life into the one who ate.
I think they almost had it right. My life
extends, a tropic vision, full of youth
and light. Their bodies wind me backwards,
strip out years of gray and wives—now look
how lovely I've become, how clean, how new.

PREGNANCY TEST

I didn't panic until I knew
it had all come out right.
Then the slide to the floor,
the breath in quick spurts.
Feeling leeched from my left hand
as though I had been sleeping on it,
as though I had only just woken up.

The indignity of it comes back to me
every time I pass the dollar store in Parkdale,
ringed out front with unshaven men and hungry dogs.
Inside the shelves are clean and bright.
I wandered the aisles, pretending
I was looking for anything else: a spatula,
poster paint, a bright plastic pail, the kind
children use to build sandcastles—
I bought three, in case I had to check again.
All the way home I bounced over potholes
on my rickety bike, still unsure
which part of my body was planning to betray me.

CURES FOR LONELINESS

After the movie look out at the glittering buildings.
Let your friends wait for the streetcar without you
and walk home. When it trundles past, look up
at the lit-up windows flashing by but there's only
a dog, head out, looking back at you.

Then it starts to drizzle. Pull your cardigan
over your head even though you know
it's a lost cause. Don't walk any faster.

There was always a storm coming—
you could taste it, nitrogen on your tongue.

Make an OKCupid account. Claim
it's because your friends made you.
Print out all the messages of five words or less
on sheets of scrap paper. Burn them
with the dried herbs of the plants you couldn't grow.
Give the pepper grinder two sharp turns
and repeat the incantation. Any incantation;
it doesn't matter. Take the ashes down to Lake Ontario
and toss them, standing out of the wind.

Boil two frogs.
Say, at least the frogs are together.

Read old love letters. Read your old journals.
If it's drivel you're writing now, well,
at least it's an improvement.

Put on a summer dress and walk through the park.
There is very little a summer dress can't cure.
When you walk past the ice cream truck, think about bacteria.
When you walk past the couple kissing on a bench, think about divorce.

Consider taking up tennis. You could be good at it
and never have known. You could practice
by hitting balls against the wall.

Sleep like a starfish.
How could you ever give up so much space?

Go out walking in the mornings. Drink coffee.
Look at pictures of ex-lovers on Instagram.
Criticize his new girlfriend's haircut. Look at porn
where the woman is smiling, but the man's face
is always out of frame. Admire the ribbons
wrapped around her wrists. Wear them in your hair.

SO I DID SIT AND EAT

Rings on her hands except
where it matters—

perhaps it reminds him,
perhaps he has been meaning to

magazine beautiful, ethnically ambiguous
with a streak of gray

the kind whose purpose is just to remind you
how gracefully she's aging, how real her hair

if anyone believes they deserve this
surely it is them

surely their hearts don't tick out
their list of disqualifying sins

ten years in the future, no vengeful ghost
with an unpaid ticket

for the original crime

IN THE BOTANICAL GARDENS OF VALENCIA

The cat leapt onto the bench
where I happened to be sitting, watery and wretched,
and suddenly grateful: never an animal person but
it's true, what they say, the intuition.
Dogs go mad in the weeks before earthquakes,
furious, terrified; my old roommate's cat
would army-crawl across the apartment
in the hours before a storm, more reliable
than the Weather Channel.

Having worked myself into an overwrought state
re: the kindness of animals, who recognized
the animal part of myself, panicking—
what's been left undone, the chasm
wide enough to fall into—the cat, just as calmly,
flicked its stray self off and away from me.

This was after I had gotten lost in the city,
and after wandering the medical section of the gardens
with the poisons fenced off and three languages
warning you not to touch, but just there, it would be so easy.

The indifference of the animal was the truer comfort.
Like a garden, it has its own concerns:
where it will sleep, whether it will eat. I am
useless and uninteresting to a hungry cat;
it doesn't care that I am crying, or whether
I am too dangerous to touch.

AGAINST FATE

Not believing in soulmates, nonetheless
it's a marvel how far back we'd have to go
to set the whole thing in motion:

somehow your grandmother had to survive,
blue-eyed and skeletal. My birth
required a farm accident, an unmarriageable ancestor

gone to college, finding another soldier boy.
An arm makes a petty sacrifice
but there were more:

one of your lives laid down
like a gift you never meant to return
though it carried you across the ocean

and in a way I suppose I'm grateful.
Thank you to the love before me.
Thank you to the wine and bread

my mother starved for, uprooted us for,
all bringing me to the city by the lake
where I waited. Goodnight, someone.

That first afternoon, I thought,
My life could change, and then
you were walking toward me with the sun behind you

and you were kind. That's all.
There were a thousand other things that had to happen
and a thousand other people we each could have met

and since I am a practical person, I believe
I could have been as happy with any of them,
although I can't imagine how.

SOMEWHERE BETWEEN ME AND THE DESERT

There's a trick to it, the twenty-nine bullets
shimmering to the floor.
You could use a screwdriver.
You could use a different part of the gun.

How best to telegraph my harmlessness:
arms extended, blood still pumping
through the chambers of the heart.
Palms out: away from my body, away from yours.
The universal signal, the hope for recognition
across a great distance. How long would it take?
To see whether I was a danger to him?

He says he was never a good shot.
He says after dark, the sky arced with red light.

There's boredom, mostly, then panic,
then boredom again. I grew up
between the ocean and the desert.
Then I opened a book and saw it: that other sea.

The grime-streaked children. The helicopters lifting off,
a whirl of dust. I don't know what it sounds like
when you stand that close. It's only cinematic:
the boots, the guns, the pregnant woman
walking towards the border
with nothing and nothing behind her.

In class, we divided into two camps. As an exercise.
That was when he was learning his party trick, with the screwdriver.

I don't know what sound it makes, the bullet in the chamber.

SEVEN BRIEF LESSONS ON PHYSICS

with thanks to Carlo Rovelli

THE MOST BEAUTIFUL OF THEORIES

Time passes more quickly in the mountains.
Not a romanticism, but a fact—
the higher you are, the faster it all goes.

Down in the desert there is a fraction of a fraction more.
You could wander out alone and see
the curvature of space streaking overhead.
The Milky Way like a veil pulled back.
Behind it, another veil.

Imagine a universe of tiny grains. Imagine infinity.
The grains are not the mystery.
Reality is only in movement—
the quantum leap, from existence to nothing.

Each of them began with such hesitance.
To the last, such doubt.
Imagine the particle wave of the mind
as it moves from hesitance to doubt.
Whether it looks like certainty is not the mystery.

Imagine a box of light.
Imagine a light year through the curve of time.
We only exist reaching from one thing
to the next. The reaching
is not the mystery. The box of light
is not the mystery.

First it blew outward.
Then we were very small
in a very great sea.

The sky is not above us.
Nor are we above the earth.

PARTICLES

Here, something you may find comforting:
there is no such thing as a void.
There are particles in every dark space
writing the cosmic alphabet.

In the muscle of your heart, in its own
black hole, they are rearranging themselves.
They are going to tell you a story.

There are two ways of explaining the world.
They cannot both be right, but
both of them are right. (Very well.)

So: an impasse. An abyss. A doubling of thought.

You already know that only heat moves.
One hand to another. A cold spoon in a warm cup.
But it's sheer chance that it happens this way.
It is less likely that a hot thing grows hotter,
but not impossible.

Further, this is the only way to experience the passage of time.
Which is different depending on your standing in the world.
If it does not move from place to place,
for a moment it does not exist.
It is holding out of time.

You may already know this, from your understanding of the world.
You may have experienced luck.

It could be that our brains are computers.
Then the question of free will,
asked over and over.
It could be a complex system of neurons,
brief flares, creating heat and time.
It could be a box of light.

THE ASTRONAUT, ON RETURNING TO EARTH

The world is bright and noisy. That's the first
I miss, my quiet capsule in the sky,
the silent hum of universe and stars,
the quick rotation of the rising sun.
It rose each ninety minutes. Here on earth
the days stretch long, unable to be filled
with food, with water, playgrounds, garbage cans.
The cacophony of shouting, sirens,
yowling cats, the neighbours having sex through
thinning walls—if only I could stuff my ears
with cotton, or turn the birdsong volume down.
Or be up there, my elemental womb.
On Twitter they would ask to see their towns,
the way they fit together on the earth.
It's narcissism, yes, but also sweet
and hopeful: that we're none of us alone.
The beauty has been spoken of before,
the small blue marble rolling in my fist.
The rapid-fire sunrise/sunsets, too,
were lovely, as we rolled across the sky.
To look the other way, we rarely did.
There wasn't time; we had too much to do.
And anyway there wasn't much to see.
And once, outside, I found I could let go.

EPITHALAMIUM

First, let me send my regrets.

Later on I'll pore over the pictures
like a detective in a darkroom
but with a few modern advantages,
clicking my way closer.

You argued about what you wore.
That I know from her.

You wore no jacket. Her dress
would never suit me, and thank god.
I'm trying to remember the ring—

the story you didn't tell—

but fortunately there's only one thing
we have in common.

Three years later it's like I'm there,
running my fingers over the seams
like I'll be able to crack the safe.
But there's no secret to it.

Would anyone object? Not me, even now.
All of it had to happen exactly so.
I'm not there, not in any pictures,
not even in a corner, waiting my turn.

WHAT I'LL TELL YOU

I have cried only for selfish reasons:
in pain, physical or otherwise
only rarely for the heart fictional
or grieving

I have been wasteful, throwing away
what ought to have been composted
I have declined to rinse the recycling
I have contributed to the destruction of the earth

I have gossiped, and gladly,
seeing the door
unlock in front of me
I have stretched the truth wide enough
to make it whole

I have lied to my father
I have cursed God ever after
I have stopped believing
I have taken what did not belong to me

I have said no to everything
until now

THE LAST JEALOUSY

is for the conversations at the end, the failed ones
of a kind we never hope to have

that stretched on for hours, during which
you were not available to me, you were with her—

during the slow dismantling, the fraying
of the canopy, in low voices.

You didn't argue, although I've been jealous
of those too, and all the cities in which the arguments took place,

exotic ones: I am jealous of the food you never ate in Prague,
of all your unhappy nights in Berlin, they are something

I can't touch, even now; try as I might
you have gone on being patient, you refuse to let me see

what it might look like: your heartbreak,
what your face looks like

when the door is finally closed, I
want every piece of it, yes: even this.

THE BATS

All week we'd lain in the sun
half-dreaming. Mint leaves
and lime buds caught in our teeth.
Mostly we avoided children, but once
you'd pointed—maybe in a few years.
The girl was sleeping, head slung
over her father's shoulder and one hand dangling.

On the last night we took two water glasses
and a bottle of cheap champagne
to the edge of the pool. The moon
gave enough light to see by.

Now and then a bat dipped low
over the green fluorescent pool
and the surface broke, but only for a second
until it hurtled forward, a discordant flapping
towards the moon, wing after wing
after bright uneven wing.

NEEDLE

I was happy so of course
I looked for something to ruin

some proof that disaster
was already knit too many rows back
to unravel and save

the slipped stitch, the blinked-open gap
to poke a finger through and widen

what comes through is daylight
from another room and the water
running in another kitchen sink
where another pair of soapy hands

are lifting it up,
twisting out the water,
wringing its soft neck.

VIENNA

After James Fenton

All Tuesday morning you could catch me dreaming
despite the gleaming spreadsheets on my screen
of a church and spires reaching
towards a sky that I've been teaching
you is blue there in Vienna
when that's where I'll be with you.

Don't talk to me of schnitzel
or the hungry childish fits I'll
be throwing when the coffee's hard to find.
Somehow you won't mind.
I'll be in Vienna. You too?

That dark red gargantuan wheel
in the park, the behemoth of steel
that opens its hands.
Who cares where we land!
We'll be in Vienna, we two.

The ticket I read and reread, to be certain
of the dates and the facts and the plane that we'll flirt in
and maybe we won't go out
until late in the day, two great louts
when I'm in Vienna with you.

I don't mean to complicate you.
I just want to date and date you
and keep going like that
till we're both laid out flat.
I'll go to Vienna with you.

MEDIZINHISTORISCHES MUSEUM

Disease and malformation, rotten luck:
the hearts suspended on display, with knees
and kidneys, arteries with chalky builds
and dye thread through to show the ruined valve.
A single eyeball in a viscous goo
where filaments of vision wave behind.

How many million things can still go wrong:
legs fused together in a mermaid farce,
two faces on one skull that never meet
and never look into the other's eyes.
No feet or brains or once-inflated lungs.
A few rows back, a uterus and tubes,
one tiny damaged face and window out.

MAKEUP

You can fill in the gaps with your fingers,
small circles, and always moving upward.
The goal is light, the crack that lets youth in
and lifts it like an offering. Here sits
the altar, topped with frankincense and myrrh,
your flat face in the mirror looking blank,
half-done. A sunset's options spread before you,
a daily mask, an ornamental sheen.

Behind you in the mirror there's a shadow,
a ghost girl whose small frame has not arrived
but whom you can imagine, aping lipstick
to her mouth, the smell of your perfume
that smells to her of safety, glamour, home.

And though you'll say she doesn't need to wear it
she thinks her mother's beauty rivals all
the mortal women who have sat here, preening
into a glass that never feints or lies,
but lets you change your face like an enchantment:
a sweep of shadow over both your eyelids;
the lipstick takes the colour from your mouth.

TIDE OVER

I'm thinking all the time what it'd be like,
the belly swollen, tidal turn of moon.
One cup a day, then decaf, watching you
brew separate pots, since this is the one thing
I'll have to do alone. Not absentee:
you'd be there for each grainy ultrasound,
each diaper class, the baby CPR.
But when the foot kicks out there's only one
soft bladder it connects with. Flesh distraught,
my breasts unrecognizable to both.
Small alien that's chosen me for host.
Skin taut, now loose, in this, the great exhaling.
Sea-change inside, moon-conjured, amniotic,
first creature that could wash to shore and crawl.

KIPPAH

The penis is the only thing left
to fight about, little mushroom cap,
little mark of godliness.

No baptism, no holy water
pouring from his grandmother's hands
writing the blank check of salvation.

No bar mitzvah either, no rabbi,
no wine and vampiric ritual
enacted on my eight-day-old child.

We'd name him after his grandfather.
We'd light candles on Friday evenings
and make up a prayer.

He cannot explain why he wants this one thing
which inclines me to grant it, this severing
of the crown, this gift of family blood.

CONTRACTION

Flat belly the sorrow of my future self.
Empty like a curb-stomped can.
Tense with waiting

like a party when you're still not sure
if any guests will arrive. Stretched
streamer. Deflated balloons.

Puffed out with air, the distended image
and the physics of it, the impossibility.
Biological—well, a man said that.

I would eat no sushi, I would drink no wine.
Bovine vitamins. Morning Saltines.
Warm hands waiting for the kick,

the tick of a crocodile's jaws.
Begging for the plane landing on my roof.
Shrapnel in the walls.

Never so concentrated before.
For a long time there wasn't any face,
but now there is a face.

IF LUCK

Late night and feigning sleep
in the back of our maroon minivan
while the streetlights passed over me
line after sodium line long after
I had given up trying to read in pieces

Then nosing into the garage
and my father unbuckling my seatbelt
and lifting me up and carrying me into the house
my eye cracked open to survey the house at intervals:
flash of fireplace, kitchen ceiling, parquet floor

Last road trip I twisted around the passenger seat
and I could see them: the ghost children,
blinking at me or squabbling in the back seat,
if I am very lucky and they come to me,
and if they pretend to sleep I will be very lucky,
unbuckling their small bodies and carrying them into the house
where, if they are lucky, they will fall
from the pretend sleep into the real
and I will watch them dreaming, remembering
when I had only dreamed of them.

ACKNOWLEDGEMENTS

Thank you to the editors of the following, in which versions of these poems first appeared: *The Antigonish Review, Arc, The Claremont Review, CV2, The Dalhousie Review, Event, Existere, The Hart House Review, The Literary Review of Canada, Poetry is Dead, Poetry Lives Here, Prairie Fire, The Rusty Toque, Scarborough Fair*, and the *University of Toronto Alumni Magazine*.

For inspiring some of these poems, thank you to Lorna Crozier, Carlo Rovelli, and James Fenton. Thank you to Denis De Klerck, for his support of these poems in particular and poetry in Canada in general.

Thank you to my parents, who have loved me unconditionally even when it became clear that I was going to write about my childhood. Thank you to my brothers, Adam and Braden, and my sister-in-law Kristin, for their continuing support.

For her earliest encouragement, thank you to my high school English teacher, Nancy Knol. Thank you to Mahak Jain and Marcia Walker, curators of the Emerging Writers Reading Series in Toronto, where several of these poems were read in 2018. Thank you to Elise Partridge, Phoebe Wang, Daniel Scott Tysdal, and David O'Meara and my cohort at Banff in 2012, for their professional support and advice. For their friendship and love over the years, thank you to Laura Harris, Theresa Klein-Horsman, and Mary Helen Gallucci-Wright.

Thank you to Penny, for not caring about any of this and for greeting me every morning with one hundred percent enthusiasm, and to Yonatan Marmor, for his encouragement and love.

Originally from Northern California, Laura spent time in Grand Rapids, Michigan and Waterloo, Ontario before settling in Toronto, where she now lives. She holds an MA in English Literature from the University of Toronto, where she won the E.J. Pratt Poetry Medal and the University of Toronto Magazine alumni poetry contest. She has been previously published widely across Canada and works in corporate communications. This is her first book.